Daisy

Daisy

by E. Sandy Powell

illustrations by
Peter J. Thornton

A BOOK ABOUT
CHILD ABUSE

CAROLRHODA BOOKS

MINNEAPOLIS, MINNESOTA   USA

Thanks to Annalise
— P. J. T.

This book is available in two editions:
Library binding by Carolrhoda Books, Inc.
Soft cover by First Avenue Editions
241 First Avenue North
Minneapolis, Minnesota 55401

Library of Congress Cataloging-in-Publication Data

Powell, E. Sandy.
  Daisy / by E. Sandy Powell ; illustrations by Peter J. Thornton.
  p.   cm.
  Summary: A young girl deals with the emotional and physical
problems of being a victim of child abuse.
  ISBN 0-87614-449-0 (lib. bdg.)
  ISBN 0-87614-543-8 (pbk.)
  [1. Child abuse—Fiction.] I. Thornton, Peter, 1956-   ill.
II. Title.
PZ7.P87715Dai   1991
[E]—dc20   90-48223
                                                     CIP
                                                      AC

Manufactured in the United States of America

1 2 3 4 5 6 7 8 9 10 00 99 98 97 96 95 94 93 92 91

To Diane

It's hard to tell someone if you're being abused. I know. I didn't tell anyone until I was eight, and then I hated talking about it. Now I'm nine and I'm glad I told. My dad doesn't hurt me or hit me anymore.

We used to live in a broken-down house 10 blocks from school. The long walk home was my "treasured time." That's when I looked for new things to draw, like the outline of an oak tree against the sky or the shape of a house with a fancy porch.

I don't think anybody knew I was collecting pictures in my mind. And I don't think anybody noticed that I was sucking in air between my teeth, saving up extra for the night. At home I had trouble breathing.

After school, I was never sure if my dad was going to be home or not. When he wasn't, I'd do my chores quickly by pretending I was caught in an ogre's castle. If I emptied the ashtrays and got supper ready on time, the ogre might leave me alone. Then I could draw before going to bed.

But sometimes my dad would be home. That meant they didn't need him at work. "What took you so long?" he'd holler. "Lazy Daisy, just like a roadside weed!" That's how he talked to me when he'd been drinking. "Why didn't you clean up the kitchen this morning? Now get in there and finish it!" I couldn't pretend when he yelled at me.

I knew he was just mad about work, so I'd wash up his lunch dishes without saying anything. Then I'd make him a cup of coffee. Sometimes he'd stop yelling if he had coffee. He might even hold me on his lap. Once or twice we played ticktacktoe. Then it was like the king had returned and the ogre was gone forever!

Usually, though, I'd do something awful and spoil our good time, like when I poured rotten milk in his coffee, or when I accidentally burned the hamburgers. "Daisy! You're so stupid. How'd I get such a dumb one? *Dumb* Daisy, that's what your mother should've named you. That's probably why she left. She could see you were growing up stupid."

When my dad got to talking about Momma, I really had to be careful.

Once I made us toasted cheese sandwiches. I even cut them into smiley faces like we did at school. But when I got the platter on the table, my dad didn't smile at all. "What've you done to our dinner?" he demanded. "You know we can't waste money prettying up food. That's just the kind of thing your mother would've done, and I won't have you being like her!" He smashed the platter, then yelled at me to clean it up.

I was bending over so I didn't see. Maybe my dad meant to kick the table, but he kicked me instead. I don't think he wanted to hurt me, because the blood on my forehead made him even madder. "Daisy, you're so clumsy, so stupid and clumsy! Now you've gone and had an accident. You ought to be glad I don't take you to the hospital." When he said *hospital,* his eyes changed and he hunkered down in front of me. "Daisy, you listen to me, and listen good. That was an accident, you hear? If anybody thought it wasn't an accident, the authorities would come and take you away." I didn't know who "authorities" were, but they sounded way worse than ogres.

I still hate the smell of toasted cheese sandwiches because that's when the hitting began. My dad didn't hit me very often, mostly on the days that they sent him home from work. Drawing pictures made me feel better then. I'd draw a beautiful queen kissing the ogre to turn him into a king.

Once my dad found the queen pictures and made me explain. I didn't want to, but I couldn't lie to him. For days after that he waited for me to get home from school. "D-A-I-S-Y," he'd say in his singsongy voice, "did you draw any pictures today? The ogre wants to see them." Then he'd laugh real scarylike while he drank his beer. I never said *he* was the ogre. Why did he tease me so much? Even though I tried to be good, I always did something wrong.

My dad kept warning me to be quiet about what went on at home. I didn't talk much at school anyway. And after that first kick, he made sure to hit me only on places my clothes would cover. I wore long-sleeved sweaters a lot. Nobody saw the bruises.

But things changed when Mrs. Calley volunteered as a tutor in our class. At first I just read to her during tutoring. Then I got to pretending she was my fairy godmother, and I told her stories about the ogre. When the teacher bragged about my drawings, Mrs. Calley nodded real big. "I could tell right away," Mrs. Calley said, "that Daisy-girl is somebody worth knowing!"

I didn't bother telling them that I'd stopped drawing.

Then my dad lost his job, so he was always home. Once I told him as nicely as I could that we didn't have any food in the house. Even though he wasn't really drunk, he almost exploded. He grabbed my hair and pulled me to the cupboards. "Don't tell me there's nothing to eat, you ungrateful kid!" he yelled. "There's cereal right there in front of you!" I poured some into a bowl and tried not to choke. The cereal was old and dry, and we didn't have any milk.

At night when the little girl cried in bed, the ogre came and hit her, over and over.

I thought I got all the black spots covered, but that morning in tutoring, Mrs. Calley said, "He hurts you, doesn't he?"

"No!" I said, and I ran out of the room. I went back to class instead of to tutoring.

The next morning, even though it wasn't my turn, the teacher sent me to see Mrs. Calley. "Hi, Daisy-girl," she smiled.

I hardly sat down before she started in again about my dad. "You know how I knew?" she asked. "Because my papa used to hurt me. Not a sometimes spanking or scolding, but real bad hurts." She pulled up her sleeve and showed me a scar. "This is abuse, Daisy."

"My dad doesn't do anything," I said. But inside I wished that I knew who authorities were. If Mrs. Calley was an authority, I'd go ahead and tell.

That afternoon, the sky was spooky with the trees all dark. I had decided never to draw again, but a quick sketch of the shadows wouldn't really be drawing. Since my dad was banging around in the kitchen, I tiptoed into my room.

I got so busy with the shading that I didn't hear him come in. I heard the thud on my back, though, even before I felt it. My chest knocked into the table, and the pencils and paper went flying. Then my dad yanked my shoulder around and hit across my face. He must've gone crazy— that's how he looked—because he'd never hit me in the face before. "You're not going to draw, ever, do you hear? Look where it got your mother—she should've stayed! If you want something to do, young lady, you can pick up where you left off—in the kitchen!" He slammed the door on his way out of the house.

I could barely crawl over to my bed. I thought I was going to die. Even with my sleeping bag pulled up, I shivered all night long.

There's no way to cover a black eye. When Mrs. Calley saw me the next morning, she took me straight to the tutoring room. "Now that's all I can take, Daisy-girl! There's no worse hurt than being hurt by your family. Child, I know. It happened to me. When Papa hit me, my mama wouldn't stop him. You see, Daisy, if I don't help you, I'll be just like her." Mrs. Calley reached out and touched my arm. "You have to tell, Daisy. Either tell me, or your teacher, or your principal, or a neighbor. Please, let someone help you."

I didn't mean to cry. I usually didn't. But once I started, I couldn't stop.

We went to the principal and I told them both everything. The principal's voice was gentle. "There's one thing I want you to remember," she said. "None of this is your fault. Your father has a problem and needs special people to help him. He's been wrong to hurt you, Daisy, but none of this is your fault." I stopped crying.

Back in the tutoring room, Mrs. Calley told me about her dad. "The authorities took Papa to a treatment center for his drinking. Then he went to classes to learn how to stop hitting. I stayed with my aunt for three years, off and on, but when I moved back home, Papa was all better. He still yelled some, but he never hit me again."

"Your dad might get better, or he might not," said Mrs. Calley. "That's up to him. If he doesn't, the authorities will find you a new home, a new patch of ground for you to take root in, some place with warmth and love.

"I wish we were rich," I said, "then my dad wouldn't get mad and hit me."

"It doesn't matter if you have enough money or not. If people were hurt when they were little, it's really hard for them not to hurt their own children."

"Do you think that's why my dad hits me?"

"It could be, Daisy. It could be."

I thought I wouldn't be afraid of the authorities and all, since I had Mrs. Calley to talk to. Right away I went to live with a family over on the other side of school. They had a four-year-old girl, a cat, and colored pencils. I wanted to ask Mrs. Calley if it was okay that I only felt a little bit better, even though the people I lived with were nice. I was scared that my dad wasn't getting help. And I didn't know who would clean up for him, without me there.

But Mrs. Calley wasn't at school the next day, or the day after that. My teacher said Mrs. Calley would be back, but when she wasn't there the rest of the week, I was really scared. I felt so alone!

All I wanted to do on Saturday was watch TV. My foster mom let me all morning long. But in the afternoon, I got a letter.

Dear Daisy,
  I had to leave school in a hurry because my mother is ill. She's getting better and I'll be home soon.
  Don't you forget now, child, when you feel alone, or scared and unsure, you just hold your head up high, and tell yourself what I think of you. Do you remember? *That Daisy, she's somebody worth knowing!*
        Your friend always,

  Mrs. Calley

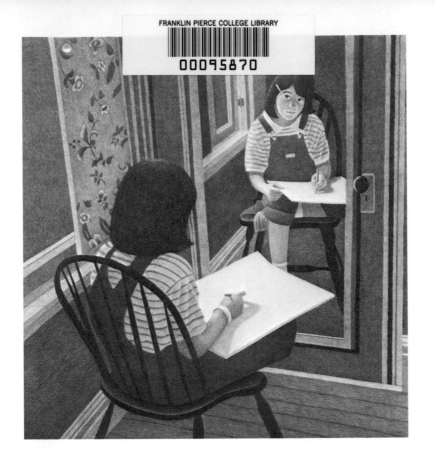

I was sure Mrs. Calley would understand about watching TV all morning if I needed to. The more I thought about her, though, the more I wanted to draw. I had an idea for just the picture I wanted to give Mrs. Calley.

I'd never tried to draw myself before.